MW01521072

Go Vertical

21 Days to An Improved Prayer Life

Iann Schonken

Copyright © 2015 by Iann Schonken

All rights reserved. No part of this publication may be reproduced, distributed or transmitted in any form or by any means, without prior written permission.

Iann Schonken

420 N. El Camino Real

Oceanside, CA 92058

www.iannschonken.com

Dedication

To my precious wife Melodi and our three boys: You are my inspiration!

To my beloved church family and readers everywhere: Let us use our prayers to change our world!

Contents

Acknowledgements

A special thank you to Melodi, my wife and life partner, who kept on encouraging me to finish this book on prayer, which has been on the back burner for a long time!

IANN SCHONKEN

Why I Wrote This Book

I have always felt saddened by the unnecessary guilt people feel the moment the topic of prayer comes up in a conversation. It seems like they believe that they will never be good enough and pray long enough to experience delight in prayer. But talking to your heavenly Father should be a delight and something you can look forward to! Don't you agree?

For many believers, their prayer lives have become a desolate battleground of personal failure. This is so unnecessary! A few slight adjustments can lift your chin as you look into the loving eyes of your heavenly Father!

In this book, I have compiled twenty-one principles to help you enter this wide-open, expansive world of joyful prayer. For the next twenty-one days, do one thing extra every day as you journey through different instructions from the Bible. Resist the temptation to rush ahead and finish this book in a single setting. Rather, savor the day's lesson and allow yourself to ponder its implications. Then, the next day, when you add a new strategy, you will not forget the previous day's lesson.

At first it will feel like a new discipline, but you will quickly break through into pure delight. Sooner than you think, you will enjoy your prayer journey with God! Thank you for reading!

~ *Iann Schonken*

DAY 1

Prayer Is Simply Talking to God

"What a friend we have in Jesus, all our sins and griefs to bear! What a privilege to carry everything to God in prayer! O what peace we often forfeit, O what needless pain we bear, all because we do not carry everything to God in prayer." Hymn lyrics by Joseph M. Scriven (1820-1886).

From the beginning, God was close to man. He did not only shape man and breathe into man, but He actively talked to man on a regular basis. When man sinned in the Garden of Eden, God came looking for man, calling out to re-establish the connection that was so precious to God. God wanted to talk about what went wrong and how they could go forward in the best possible way. God wanted to fix what broke their fellowship, and took the initiative to seek out man to bridge the gap caused by disobedience.

To this day, God desires to be in conversation with you, His most precious creation. Prayer is many things, but first, it is a heartfelt and honest conversation between you and God about what matters in your life. You live in a world with limitations, and you have unique needs as you travel through your life. God cares about your life, and He is waiting for you to open the channels of communication. Jesus makes it clear that God is waiting for you to start talking, without hesitation, about what you need from Him:

> *"Don't bargain with God. Be direct. Ask for what you need. This isn't a cat-and-mouse, hide-and-seek game we're in. If your child asks for bread, do you trick him with sawdust? If he asks for fish, do you scare him with a live snake on his plate? As bad as you are, you wouldn't think of such a thing. You're at least decent to your own children. So don't you think the God who conceived you in love will be even better?"* Matthew 7:7-11 (The Message Bible).

Our scripture of the day makes it clear: Ask for what you need! Would you just try it today, maybe even right now? Talking to God is just like talking to your best friend ... only better. But what kind of friend will never respond to your words? True conversation is a two-way street.

> *"A man prayed, and at first he thought that prayer was talking. But he became more and more quiet until, in the end, he realized that prayer is listening."* Soren Kierkegaard

God is willing and able to help you. Just start talking to God about your fears, your needs, and your dreams. He is politely and patiently waiting for you. Will you take the first step? Then, are you willing to wait for His response … the quiet whispers of His friendly voice?

Prayer is simply talking and listening to God.

Action Step:

- What is the biggest obstacle you face right now?

- What are you most concerned about?

- Write it down somewhere.

- Take a few minutes to talk to God about this challenge and ask for His help in a specific way. Imagine asking Him like a little kid asking an adult for assistance with a difficult task. You will be so glad you did!

Review:

1. Prayer Is Simply Talking and Listening to God.

IANN SCHONKEN

DAY 2

Prayer Should Flow from A Contrite Heart

"Have we trials and temptations? Is there trouble anywhere? We should never be discouraged; take it to the Lord in prayer. Can we find a friend so faithful, who will all our sorrows share? Jesus knows our every weakness; take it to the Lord in prayer." Hymn lyrics by Joseph M. Scriven (1820-1886).

"Then if my people who are called by my name will humble themselves and pray and seek my face and turn from their wicked ways, I will hear from heaven and will forgive their sins and restore their land." 2 Chronicles 7:14 (New Living Translation).

While it is true that we should feel comfortable in approaching God in prayer, we should remember that

God is holy and we are not. God is perfect in all His ways, and we, as humans, are flawed due to our limitations. We need His forgiveness on a regular basis.

However, our mistakes and sins are provided for in what Jesus had done for us in His death and resurrection. Thus, we can approach God with a humble confidence that we have been forgiven for what had once separated us from Him.

Jesus tells a story of two men who approached God in prayer (Luke 18:9-14). The one was superior in his attitude to the point of thanking God that he was not as bad as the other man next to him. The second man came with a broken and contrite heart, recognizing his frailties and sins in the presence of a holy God. Jesus taught that God heard the second man's prayers, while the prayers of the first man went unanswered.

Today's lesson aims to remind you that we should never have a superior or lackadaisical attitude when we approach God. He deserves our respect, reverence and undivided attention. Check out what the prophet Isaiah wrote about people who come to God with a humble and contrite heart:

> *"The high and lofty one who lives in eternity, the Holy One, says this: 'I live in the high and holy place with those whose spirits are contrite and humble. I restore the crushed spirit of the humble and revive the courage of those with*

repentant hearts.'" Isaiah 57:15 (New Living Translation).

God wants to restore whatever may be lacking in your life. He wants to revive your weary soul, but it is important to come to Him with contrite and humble hearts.

Action Step:

- Can you think of a time when you talked to God in a flippant attitude? Maybe you were not paying attention or giving God your full attention as you spoke to Him?

- Can you see from the scriptures above that God rewards those who approach Him with the proper respect and awe?

- Let's agree that from now on we will not only talk to God, but we will also make sure to pay attention to the way in which we talk to Him. With God, your attitude is important.

Review:

1. Prayer Is Simply Talking and Listening to God.

2. Prayer Should Flow from A Contrite Heart.

IANN SCHONKEN

DAY 3

Your Prayers Should Be Confident

"So let us come boldly to the throne of our gracious God. There we will receive his mercy, and we will find grace to help us when we need it most." Hebrews 4:16 (New Living Translation)

You must be confident in the goodness of God. If God is a good God, which He is, and if He cares deeply about us, which He does, why would He not receive us as we approach His throne? Why would you expect anything less than a positive reception and a generous response to your requests from a good God?

The scripture above makes it clear that a confident conversation with God will result in mercy and grace. Confident prayer will have amazing results! In fact,

Jesus taught His disciples that they could expect joy because of their prayers to God the Father:

> *"You haven't done this before. Ask, using my name, and you will receive, and you will have abundant joy."* John 16:24 (New Living Translation).

We should be excited to talk to God, and we can have high expectations about the results of our prayers! God loves to see us approach Him with confidence because it shows that we think He is a good Father. Remember the scripture from our first day:

> *"You're at least decent to your own children. So don't you think the God who conceived you in love will be even better?"* Matthew 7:11 (The Message Bible).

Action Step:

- Bring your requests to God's throne in prayer with a new confidence in His goodness. Believe in His endless willingness to give you what you need today.

Review:

1. Prayer Is Simply Talking and Listening to God.

2. Prayer Should Flow from A Contrite Heart.

3. Your Prayers Should Be Confident.

DAY 4

Your Prayers Should Be Concise and To the Point

"When you pray, don't babble on and on as people of other religions do. They think their prayers are answered merely by repeating their words again and again. Don't be like them, for your Father knows exactly what you need even before you ask him." Matthew 6:7-8 (New Living Translation).

It is tempting to ramble when talking to God, because in dealing with people, we often must repeat ourselves to be understood. However, in prayer, you must get to the point and talk to God like He already knows what you need. Your objective in prayer is to invite Him into your situation as you place your trust in Him. Make a point of not saying the same thing over and over. Once you learn this simple principle, you will discover that it is truly liberating.

It will require some self-examination and self-discipline on your part at first, but that is a good thing. Your prayer times will become more effective and more meaningful.

Think about it: You would not want to ramble on and on if you should get a chance to meet the president of the United States, would you? So why ramble on when speaking to God, the Ruler of the Universe? Get to the point. Keep it simple. God is smarter than you will ever know and He is ready to help you.

Action Step:

- Present your requests to the Lord today and make sure that you do not allow any useless repetitions in your conversation with Him.

- He already knows what you need, and He just wants you to verbalize it in plain language to show your faith and dependence on Him.

Review:

1. Prayer Is Simply Talking and Listening to God.

2. Prayer Should Flow from A Contrite Heart.

3. Your Prayers Should Be Confident.

4. Your Prayers Should Be Concise and To the Point.

DAY 5

Your Prayers Should Be Consistent and Constant

"Never stop praying." I Thessalonians 5:17 (New Living Translation).

There is no circumstance or situation in which we should allow ourselves to believe that we cannot talk to God. Throughout history men and women have prayed to God in all kinds of situations. It is evident that God is always near and that He is always able to help.

Daniel prayed on the way to the lion's den, and God shut the mouths of the lions. Moses talked to God on the shores of the Red Sea and God parted the waters right on time.

Whether in good times or bad times, lean times or abundant times, early in the morning or late at night ... talking to God is not only possible, but critical to our survival! Simply put, we need to talk to God at all hours and on all occasions!

Sometimes I feel like God may not want to talk to me because I have messed up or I have had a bad attitude. Yet, it is exactly at those times I need to talk to God the most!

Please hear this today: Talk to God consistently in that you do not let a day pass without having been in conversation with Him. Talk to God constantly in that you bring Him into every significant or mundane moment of your day.

Action Step:

- See if you can remember to talk to God throughout today.

- As you drive, as you work, as you get ready to eat … include God by talking to Him. He loves to hear from you!

Review:

1. Prayer Is Simply Talking and Listening to God.

2. Prayer Should Flow from A Contrite Heart.

3. Your Prayers Should Be Confident.

4. Your Prayers Should Be Concise and To the Point.

5. Your Prayers Should Be Consistent and Constant.

DAY 6

Pray in Jesus' Name

"You didn't choose me. I chose you. I appointed you to go and produce lasting fruit, so that the Father will give you whatever you ask for, using my name." John 15:16 (New Living Translation).

"At that time you won't need to ask me for anything. I tell you the truth, you will ask the Father directly, and he will grant your request because you use my name." John 16:23 (New Living Translation).

Here we have the words of Jesus, and He says that we are to produce good fruit, or good results, as we live here on the earth. He also tells us that we can ask for what we need directly from the Father and that we will get what we need. Why? Because we present our needs in the name of Jesus.

It is not as if the words, *"in the name of Jesus"* provide magical powers to our prayers. It is not as if we can only say the phrase at the end of a prayer and then God will be obligated to do whatever we ask. We must understand that praying for things that agree with God's will is the essence of praying in Jesus' name. In other words, praying in Jesus' name means the same thing as praying according to the will of God:

> *"And we are confident that he hears us whenever we ask for anything that pleases him. And since we know he hears us when we make our requests, we also know that he will give us what we ask for."* 1 John 5:14-15 (New Living Translation).

Praying in Jesus' name is praying for things that will honor and glorify Jesus. When we ask in the name of Jesus, it means that our prayers will be accepted in the same way a prayer from Jesus himself would have been accepted! That is amazing! Doesn't that give you more confidence for your prayers to be answered?

It is sad to see Christians go without the help they need because they have not read or understood these great promises! It is all right there, within reach, if only they will read it, believe it, and act on it. The question is … will you?

Action Step:

- Go ahead and talk to God about your needs and concerns. Don't forget to end your prayer time by stating that you ask these things in the name of Jesus.

- When you ask in the name of Jesus, according to the will of God, the Father wants to bless your request with a resounding, "Yes!"

Review:

1. Prayer Is Simply Talking and Listening to God.

2. Prayer Should Flow from A Contrite Heart.

3. Your Prayers Should Be Confident.

4. Your Prayers Should Be Concise and To the Point.

5. Your Prayers Should Be Consistent and Constant.

6. Pray in Jesus' Name.

IANN SCHONKEN

DAY 7

Pray About Everything

"Are we weak and heavy laden, cumbered with a load of care? Precious Savior, still our refuge; take it to the Lord in prayer. Do thy friends despise, forsake thee? Take it to the Lord in prayer! In his arms he'll take and shield thee; thou wilt find a solace there." Hymn lyrics by Joseph M. Scriven (1820-1886).

"Don't worry about anything; instead, pray about everything. Tell God what you need, and thank him for all he has done. Then you will experience God's peace, which exceeds anything we can understand. His peace will guard your hearts and minds as you live in Christ Jesus." Philippians 4:6-7 (New Living Translation).

We live in a broken world with endless troubles and challenges as far as the eye can see. This can lead to high anxiety, especially when you spend a lot of time contemplating our human existence!

Our scripture of the day makes it clear that we do not have to waste one minute worrying and being anxious! Instead, we are told to go and talk to God about all those things that concern us. We are instructed to tell God what we need and to thank Him for everything He has done.

It is my experience that an incredible peace usually follows such an exchange with God. In a moment, that peace wraps itself around my thoughts and my heart, and I am more than able to face my day.

How is that possible? What an exchange! I gave God my concerns, and He gave me His reassuring presence. When I commit to recall all the wonderful and miraculous things the Lord had done for me, I cannot help but feel elated and motivated. Now I am ready to conquer the challenges in my day! It is hard to be a pessimist when you have a grateful heart!

Action Step:

- Are you feeling a little anxious today? Pray about it!

- Tell God what you need.

- Then take the time to thank Him for what He has already done, and what He is about to do.

- Then, get ready for God's amazing peace!

Review:

1. Prayer Is Simply Talking and Listening to God.

2. Prayer Should Flow from A Contrite Heart.

3. Your Prayers Should Be Confident.

4. Your Prayers Should Be Concise and To the Point.

5. Your Prayers Should Be Consistent and Constant.

6. Pray in Jesus' Name.

7. Pray About Everything!

DAY 8

You Don't Have Because You Don't Ask

"What is causing the quarrels and fights among you? Don't they come from the evil desires at war within you? You want what you don't have, so you scheme and kill to get it. You are jealous of what others have, but you can't get it, so you fight and wage war to take it away from them. Yet you don't have what you want because you don't ask God for it." James 4:1-2 (New Living Translation).

How can it be so simple? All we should do is ask God? I thought we all must go out and compete and fight and claw our way over others until we finally can earn what we need! That's what this world wants us to believe as we fight each other for limited opportunities and resources.

But there seems to be a better way in God's Kingdom. God has no scarcity in His warehouses, and whatever is missing He can create or summon with a whisper. He can produce it from a rock or multiply a little boy's lunch to feed a multitude.

Maybe it is because we see other people, our jobs, our environment or country as our source. When the economy tanks, we begin to scheme, fight, fuss and claw. All we should do, though, is go to our true Source, God, in prayer, asking Him for what we need!

Action Step:

- What is it you think you need?

- Have you fallen into the common trap of looking to other people to give it to you?

- Have you asked God for it?

- If you haven't, ask Him now.

Review:

1. Prayer Is Simply Talking and Listening to God.

2. Prayer Should Flow from A Contrite Heart.

3. Your Prayers Should Be Confident.

4. Your Prayers Should Be Concise and To the Point.

5. Your Prayers Should Be Consistent and Constant.

6. Pray in Jesus' Name.

7. Pray About Everything!

8. You Do Not Have Because You Don't Ask God.

DAY 9

Asking God with The Wrong Motive Doesn't Work

"And even when you ask, you don't get it because your motives are all wrong—you want only what will give you pleasure. You adulterers! Don't you realize that friendship with the world makes you an enemy of God? I say it again: If you want to be a friend of the world, you make yourself an enemy of God." James 4:3-4 (New Living Translation).

God does not sponsor selfish pursuits of self-indulgent pleasures. Our Heavenly Father wants to see us mature beyond being selfish to living selfless lives of service. While He does not deny us our basic human needs of food, shelter, and clothing, He does not want us to be involved in trivial pursuits.

The things of this world should become less and less important, and the quest of the Kingdom should become our own. The quest of the Kingdom is to bring glory to the King by loving Him and loving people. It is not about loving our pleasure, but rather to serve our neighbors in the name of the Lord by sharing His Good News and eternal love.

Consider your recent talks with the Lord. Determine if you were more focused on your wants and pleasures than on your true needs as a child in God's Kingdom. Again, there are wants, and there are needs, and the mature believer can discern the difference.

God loves us, and He does not mind providing the occasional treat. Our prayers should flow from a pure motivation to be about our Heavenly Father's business here on earth. We are in the earth, but we are not of this earth, and earthly pleasures should not dominate our conversations with the Lord.

Action Step:

- Consider your recent prayer requests.

- How many of them could be considered selfish requests to indulge in earthly pleasures? How many truly reflect the Kingdom priorities you learn about in Scripture?

- Let's recalibrate our motivations in prayer. May our motivations more accurately reflect what God would consider mature and pleasing in His sight.

Review:

1. Prayer Is Simply Talking and Listening to God.

2. Prayer Should Flow from A Contrite Heart.

3. Your Prayers Should Be Confident.

4. Your Prayers Should Be Concise and To the Point.

5. Your Prayers Should Be Consistent and Constant.

6. Pray in Jesus' Name.

7. Pray About Everything!

8. You Do Not Have Because You Don't Ask God.

9. Asking God with The Wrong Motive Doesn't Work.

DAY 10

Ask Expecting to Receive from God

"If any of you lacks wisdom, let him ask of God, who gives to all liberally and without reproach, and it will be given to him. But let him ask in faith, with no doubting, for he who doubts is like a wave of the sea driven and tossed by the wind. For let not that man suppose that he will receive anything from the Lord; he is a double-minded man, unstable in all his ways." James 5:5-8 (New King James Version).

more important than anything else; supreme

Having high expectations of God in prayer is paramount. To doubt God's willingness to give is to disable our prayers. God loves to give with lavish generosity, and He loves to hear us asking Him in faith.

Our part is to ask without doubt, and His part is to give to us abundantly in His perfect timing. A doubting prayer has no chance to succeed because God expects us to be fully persuaded that He is willing and able to provide for us. Abraham understood this principle, and he received miraculous outcomes because of his faith-filled prayers:

> *"Even when there was no reason for hope, Abraham kept hoping—believing that he would become the father of many nations. For God had said to him, 'That's how many descendants you will have!' And Abraham's faith did not weaken, even though, at about 100 years of age, he figured his body was as good as dead—and so was Sarah's womb. Abraham never wavered in believing God's promise. In fact, his faith grew stronger, and in this he brought glory to God. He was fully convinced that God is able to do whatever he promises." Romans 4:18-21 (New Living Translation).*

We must be entirely convinced, like Abraham, that God can do whatever He promises! He is still a miracle-working God, and He expects us to have high expectations to be heard when we present our requests to Him in prayer.

Action Step:

- Are you fully convinced that God is not only able but willing to do what you have asked Him to do?

- Make this declaration today as you pray:

"Father God, I believe with all my heart that you are not only able, but also totally willing to help me in my areas of need. Thank you for hearing my prayers today!"

Review:

1. Prayer Is Simply Talking and Listening to God.

2. Prayer Should Flow from A Contrite Heart.

3. Your Prayers Should Be Confident.

4. Your Prayers Should Be Concise and To the Point.

5. Your Prayers Should Be Consistent and Constant.

6. Pray in Jesus' Name.

7. Pray About Everything!

8. You Do Not Have Because You Don't Ask God.

9. Asking God with The Wrong Motive Doesn't Work.

10. Ask Expecting to Receive from God.

DAY 11

Ask God to Bless Your Enemies as You Pray

"You have heard the law that says, 'Love your neighbor' and hate your enemy. But I say, love your enemies! Pray for those who persecute you! In that way, you will be acting as true children of your Father in heaven." Matthew 5:43-45 (New Living Translation)

"Bless those who persecute you. Don't curse them; pray that God will bless them." Romans 12:14 (New Living Translation).

"The eyes of the Lord watch over those who do right, and his ears are open to their prayers." 1 Peter 3:12 (New Living Translation).

To pray for those who persecute you is not easy for anyone. The most natural thing is to hurl insults at them and to talk to God about *"fixing them good!"* However, Jesus introduced a higher standard and called us to act as true children of our Father in Heaven.

Just when you think that you have figured prayer out, you are getting challenged to go to a higher level! Praying for your enemies!?

There is a promise in our scriptures we should not consider lightly. Peter writes in his letter that God's ears are especially open, or receptive, to the requests of people who do right. Do you want the Lord to hear your requests? Do what is right! What is right is to pray for your enemies, especially when it hurts the most. This kind of prayer gets the Father's attention.

In fact, Jesus is our example in praying for our enemies. He was on the cross, and, after hours of intense suffering and torture, with some of His last strength, He made time to pray for His enemies:

> *"Jesus said, 'Father, forgive them, for they don't know what they are doing.'"* Luke 23:24 (New Living Translation).

Stephen was the first Christian martyr who followed in Jesus' footsteps in praying for his enemies:

As they stoned him, Stephen prayed, "Lord Jesus, receive my spirit." He fell to his knees, shouting, "Lord, don't charge them with this sin!" And with that, he died. Acts 7:59-60 (New Living Translation).

We are all called to pray for those who despitefully use us and oppose us in life. This way we imitate Jesus and show that our Father is in heaven.

Remember to ask God to bless your enemies when you pray.

Action Step:

- Think of someone who had caused you great harm, grief or pain.

- Now ask God to bless that person and to forgive their offense against you. This will free you and free them!

Review:

1. Prayer Is Simply Talking and Listening to God.

2. Prayer Should Flow from A Contrite Heart.

3. Your Prayers Should Be Confident.

4. Your Prayers Should Be Concise and To the Point.

5. Your Prayers Should Be Consistent and Constant.

6. Pray in Jesus' Name.

7. Pray About Everything!

8. You Do Not Have Because You Don't Ask God.

9. Asking God with The Wrong Motive Doesn't Work.

10. Ask Expecting to Receive from God.

11. Ask God to Bless Your Enemies as You Pray.

IANN SCHONKEN

DAY 12

Ask the Lord to Make You More Loving

"When I think of all this, I fall to my knees and pray to the Father, the Creator of everything in heaven and on earth. I pray that from his glorious, unlimited resources he will empower you with inner strength through his Spirit. Then Christ will make his home in your hearts as you trust in him. Your roots will grow down into God's love and keep you strong. And may you have the power to understand, as all God's people should, how wide, how long, how high, and how deep his love is. May you experience the love of Christ, though it is too great to understand fully. Then you will be made complete with all the fullness of life and power that comes from God." Ephesians 3:14-19 (New Living Translation).

Paul the Apostle prayed that the Ephesian believers would understand the kind of love we are called to extend to others: the *"God kind of love."* God's love is wider, higher and deeper than we can ever truly comprehend, and it is critical to our daily lives.

In his letter to the believers at Corinth, the apostle tried to define what this love looks like and how it is supposed to operate through our lives:

> *"Love is patient and kind. Love is not jealous or boastful or proud or rude. It does not demand its own way. It is not irritable, and it keeps no record of being wronged. It does not rejoice about injustice but rejoices whenever the truth wins out. Love never gives up, never loses faith, is always hopeful, and endures through every circumstance."* I Corinthians 13:4-7 (New Living Translation).

Now, if you personalize this scripture, you may want to pray:

> *"Dear Lord, please help me to become more patient and kind. Please help me not to be jealous or boastful or proud or rude. Help me not to demand my own way and help me not to be irritable. Please help me not to keep a record of being wronged by others! Help me to rejoice whenever the truth wins out and never to rejoice over injustice. Please help me never*

to give up, never to lose faith and always to be hopeful, enduring through every circumstance that may come my way!"

Ask the Lord to make you more loving. This is the kind of prayer God loves to answer!

Action Step:

- Looking at our scriptures today, would you agree that you may need to mature into the kind of love God wants to release through you?

- Or, do you think you have "arrived?"

- Do you agree that the Lord of love will have to help you to become a more loving person?

- Be sure to ask the Lord to make you more loving regularly.

Review:

1. Prayer Is Simply Talking and Listening to God.

2. Prayer Should Flow from A Contrite Heart.

3. Your Prayers Should Be Confident.

4. Your Prayers Should Be Concise and To the Point.

5. Your Prayers Should Be Consistent and Constant.

6. Pray in Jesus' Name.

7. Pray About Everything!

8. You Do Not Have Because You Don't Ask God.

9. Asking God with The Wrong Motive Doesn't Work.

10. Ask Expecting to Receive from God.

11. Ask God to Bless Your Enemies as You Pray.

12. Ask the Lord to Make You More Loving as You Pray.

IANN SCHONKEN

DAY 13

Make Talking to God a Priority Every Day

"But I will call on God, and the Lord will rescue me. <u>Morning, noon, and night</u> I cry out in my distress, and the Lord hears my voice. He ransoms me and keeps me safe from the battle waged against me, though many still oppose me. God, who has ruled forever, will hear me and humble them." Psalm 55: 17-19 (New Living Translation).

"O Lord, God of my salvation, I cry out to you <u>by day</u>. I come to you <u>at night</u>. <u>Now</u> hear my prayer; listen to my cry." Psalm 88:1-2 (New Living Translation).

King David and Heman, the Ezrahite wrote these two portions of Scripture to show that they made prayer a priority in their lives. They made time in the middle of their distressing circumstances to meet with God and to let Him know that they need His help.

We are tempted to get so engaged with problem solving and putting out fires that we forget to invite God into our situations. Urgent things demand our immediate attention. We go into crisis mode, which exposes us to the risk of making foolish decisions. We especially need divine intervention during our crises!

If we have not already established the discipline of meeting with the Lord daily, we may get disconnected from our Heavenly Father when the bad times hit.

Talking to God must become a priority, and it is my experience that unless we schedule our priorities, they will be supplanted by other urgent, but less important things.

> *"But when you pray, go away by yourself, shut the door behind you, and pray to your Father in private. Then your Father, who sees everything, will reward you."* Matthew 6:6 (New Living Translation).

If you don't schedule a regular *"when,"* you cannot expect to have the daily rewards of answered prayers. I have three boys, and I drive them to school early in the morning. I always pray for us all as we drive out of our driveway. I pray before every meal with my family. I walk into my children's rooms at night to pray with them. We thank God for the day and ask Him for His protection during the night. I prioritize and schedule the *"when"* so that it may become normalized in our family's lifestyle.

At our church, there is a scheduled prayer meeting every day of the week early in the morning (except for Monday mornings, when our church staff rests and pray at home). Prayer should be a priority, and it only becomes a lifestyle when we schedule times of prayer at the intersections of our days.

Action Step:

- Have you made talking to God a priority in your life?

- Do you have scheduled times of prayer? How can you schedule times of prayer going forward?

Review:

1.   Prayer Is Simply Talking and Listening to God.

2.   Prayer Should Flow from A Contrite Heart.

3.   Your Prayers Should Be Confident.

4.   Your Prayers Should Be Concise and To the Point.

5.   Your Prayers Should Be Consistent and Constant.

6.   Pray in Jesus' Name.

7.   Pray About Everything!

8.   You Do Not Have Because You Don't Ask God.

9.   Asking God with The Wrong Motive Doesn't Work.

10. Ask Expecting to Receive from God.

11. Ask God to Bless Your Enemies as You Pray.

12. Ask the Lord to Make You More Loving as You Pray.

13. Make Talking to God a Priority Every Day.

IANN SCHONKEN

DAY 14

Pray According to God's Will

"And we are confident that he hears us whenever we ask for anything that pleases him. And since we know he hears us when we make our requests, we also know that he will give us what we ask for." I John 5:14-15 (New Living Translation).

God is not obligated to sponsor anything or anyone who contradicts His will and values. Jesus understood the importance of doing the Father's will. He shaped his life and ministry around pleasing God by being obedient to His will.

"For I have come down from heaven to do the will of God who sent me, not to do my own will." John 6:38 (New Living Translation).

"Father, if you are willing, please take this cup of suffering away from me. Yet I want your will to be done, not mine." Luke 22:42 (New Living Translation).

The will of God is revealed in the pages of the Bible. We must bring our requests to God with a sincere attitude of total submission to God's will. Years ago, there was an old television show called, *"Father Knows Best."* We must remind ourselves that we live the best possible lives when we desire to know and do God's will. Our Heavenly Father knows best!

Knowing God's will before we pray will require an investment of time in reading the Bible. Scripture teaches us about God's will and ways. We must try to understand what He values and what He considers worthy of His time and resources. God has priorities, and He gladly supplies us with what we need to fulfill our Kingdom responsibilities. Again, He is not obligated to sponsor and provide us with trivial things to satisfy our quest for more and more selfish pleasures.

"And even when you ask, you don't get it because your motives are all wrong—you want only what will give you pleasure. You adulterers! Don't you realize that friendship with the world makes you an enemy of God? I say it again: If you want to be a friend of the

world, you make yourself an enemy of God."
James 4:3-4 (New Living Translation).

Spend the time to find out what God wants from us as revealed in the Bible. When you ask according to the will of God, He delights in granting your requests.

Action Steps:

- Look at the things you have been asking God for lately.

- Do they contradict or confirm the values and will of God as revealed in scripture?

- In your prayer time, remind yourself of what you have read in the Bible concerning your needs. Tell yourself what God had promised you in Scripture. It will build your faith and give you confidence to ask God according to His will, and not just according to your desires.

Review:

1. Prayer Is Simply Talking and Listening to God.

2. Prayer Should Flow from A Contrite Heart.

3. Your Prayers Should Be Confident.

4. Your Prayers Should Be Concise and To the Point.

5. Your Prayers Should Be Consistent and Constant.

6. Pray in Jesus' Name.

7. Pray About Everything!

8. You Do Not Have Because You Don't Ask God.

9. Asking God with The Wrong Motive Doesn't Work.

10. Ask Expecting to Receive from God.

11. Ask God to Bless Your Enemies as You Pray.

12. Ask the Lord to Make You More Loving as You Pray.

13. Make Talking to God a Priority Every Day.

14. Pray According to God's Will.

IANN SCHONKEN

DAY 15

Prayer Frames Help Shape Our Prayers

"In this manner, therefore, pray: Our Father in heaven, hallowed be Your name. Your kingdom come. Your will be done on earth as it is in heaven. Give us this day our daily bread. And forgive us our debts, as we forgive our debtors. And do not lead us into temptation, but deliver us from the evil one. For Yours is the kingdom and the power and the glory forever. Amen."
Matthew 6:9-13 (New King James).

Jesus gave His followers this *"framework"* to assist them in their prayer lives. His intent was not necessarily to provide us with a form prayer to memorize and recite, as many believers do. Instead, it was to provide a framework to help us towards having meaningful, heartfelt talks with God. The Lord's Prayer is a guideline for prayer that can help us cover what is most important as we talk to God.

> *"All praying starts with forms of prayer ... yet relationships don't thrive on rigid communication. Relationships require originality and spontaneity."* Samuel Chadwick.

As you look at the Lord's Prayer as a framework, you see that we should ①approach God with a reverent appreciation of His holiness. Right away it is important to ②seek His will, and not our own. Then, it is appropriate to ③bring our daily needs and requests to Him. As we ④ask for the forgiveness of our sins, we acknowledge that we are required to forgive others as we receive forgiveness ourselves. Finally, we ⑤ask for God's protection from temptation and the evil that lurks in our fallen world. We end by ⑥reaffirming God as King of our universe by saying, *"For thine is the kingdom, and the power, and the glory, for ever and ever. Amen."*

In a cement project, the workers lay out the framework with wooden planks in the desired shape. Next, the cement truck is called in to fill the frame with cement. After the cement had dried, the framework of planks is removed. This is how you form what you desire to establish, whether it be a patio, a driveway or the foundation of a house.

In a similar way, the form prayer helps you shape your prayer time, and you fill it with your own words. After you have done that for a while, you can remove the prayer frame, because it had served its purpose, namely to shape and establish your prayer life. The prayer frame should never replace your heartfelt prayer times with God. After a house is built, the builders remove the scaffolding. The same with prayer frames.

We should use prayer outlines (there are many useful prayer outlines and frameworks available) to keep in mind how to approach God and what to cover. After you are well established in prayer, you should use your personal uniqueness in talking to God. The idea is to have prayers that are built on relationship and love, not just religious rites and rituals.

The prayer form gives you the confidence to start. After a while, the relationship you have established gives you the confidence to build and comfortably share your heart with God.

Action Step:

- Have you fallen into the trap of making form prayers your only way of talking to God?

- Once you have shaped your prayer time and gained a sense of how to pray, expand your time with God by adding relational conversation in your prayer times. You will find that honesty and transparency will assist you in this regard.

Review:

1. Prayer Is Simply Talking and Listening to God.

2. Prayer Should Flow from A Contrite Heart.

3. Your Prayers Should Be Confident.

4. Your Prayers Should Be Concise and To the Point.

5. Your Prayers Should Be Consistent and Constant.

6. Pray in Jesus' Name.

7. Pray About Everything!

8. You Do Not Have Because You Don't Ask God.

9. Asking God with The Wrong Motive Doesn't Work.

10. Ask Expecting to Receive from God.

11. Ask God to Bless Your Enemies as You Pray.

12. Ask the Lord to Make You More Loving as You Pray.

13. Make Talking to God a Priority Every Day.

14. Pray According to God's Will.

15. Prayer Frames Help Shape Our Prayers.

IANN SCHONKEN

DAY 16

Ask God to Change the Way You Think

"Don't copy the behavior and customs of this world, but let God transform you into a new person by changing the way you think. Then you will learn to know God's will for you, which is good and pleasing and perfect." Romans 12:2 (New Living Translation).

Many people in our world do not take the time to speak to God or to believe God for great things. They are cynical, pessimistic and toxic in their thinking, and it shows in everything they do. As believers, our challenge is that we don't always realize to what degree our thoughts have been affected by this world. Fear, doubt, and unbelief may have entered our thinking patterns over time. It can become very hard for us to pray prayers that are aligned with the "good and pleasing and perfect will of God" for us. That's why we struggle to pray for God's intervention and provision at times. Unknowingly, we have defaulted to the world's way of negative thinking.

"So then faith comes by hearing, and hearing by the word of God." Romans 10:17 NKJV

We should ask the Lord to help us as we retrain our minds by reading the Bible to think more like King's kids, rather than outcasts and rebels. When we read the Bible, we become acquainted with the ways of God and the will of God. We become better equipped to pray according to God's revealed will. We have also learned in this series of teachings that God answers prayers that are in alignment with His will. This retraining of our minds will result in us becoming new persons who can be used by God in a mighty way.

Make it a priority to pray daily for God to help you by changing the way you think about your life, your family and others. You will be so glad you did!

Action Step:

- Take a moment to inventory the way you have been thinking about your biggest challenges lately. Were you positive that God is helping you to overcome, or were you negative, thinking that all is lost and beyond repair?

- Ask God to show you in the Word how He wants to be your Good Shepherd, guarding, guiding and providing for you.

- Now pray and ask the Lord to help you by changing your thinking from tragedy to triumph; defeat to victory; and negative to positive.

- Take a moment to thank God for helping you with your thoughts.

- Your prayer results will change when you leave the world's way of thinking behind.

Review:

1. Prayer Is Simply Talking and Listening to God.

2. Prayer Should Flow from A Contrite Heart.

3. Your Prayers Should Be Confident.

4. Your Prayers Should Be Concise and To the Point.

5. Your Prayers Should Be Consistent and Constant.

6. Pray in Jesus' Name.

7. Pray About Everything!

8. You Do Not Have Because You Don't Ask God.

9. Asking God with The Wrong Motive Doesn't Work.

10. Ask Expecting to Receive from God.

11. Ask God to Bless Your Enemies as You Pray.

12. Ask the Lord to Make You More Loving as You Pray.

13. Make Talking to God a Priority Every Day.

14. Pray According to God's Will.

15. Prayer Frames Help Shape Our Prayers.

16. Ask God to Change the Way You Think.

IANN SCHONKEN

DAY 17

Think at A Higher Level When You Pray

"My thoughts are nothing like your thoughts," *says the Lord. And my ways are far beyond* *anything you could imagine. For just as the* *heavens are higher than the earth, so my ways* *are higher than your ways and my thoughts* *higher than your thoughts."* Isaiah 55:8-9 (New Living Translation).

When we pray, we approach the Maker of the universe. He simply thought about the creation of the universe, spoke it, and it was there! He obviously operates at a much higher level of power and efficiency than we can even begin to grasp with our finite minds! Therefore, when we come before Him, we must recalibrate our expectations to a higher level. We should reach beyond our "normal" to access His infinite capabilities.

We honor God when we ask Him for miraculous provisions and interventions. We dishonor Him when we limit Him by acting like He is not able to take care of us. Most of us will agree that God can help us generally, but most of the time we doubt His willingness to help us specifically. We fuss and worry, often thinking that others must be more deserving of His provision than us. Thus, we don't ask and don't receive from Him what we desperately need.

We must elevate our thinking and remind ourselves that God can change any situation with a whisper. His words never fall to the ground powerless and limp:

> *"The rain and snow come down from the heavens and stay on the ground to water the earth. They cause the grain to grow, producing seed for the farmer and bread for the hungry. It is the same with my word. I send it out, and it always produces fruit. It will accomplish all I want it to, and it will prosper everywhere I send it."* Isaiah 55:10-11 (New Living Translation).

Do you comprehend just how powerful this is? One word from God creates brand new realities and abundant resources! All He requires of us is to acknowledge that

He is all-powerful. We must approach His throne with the confident knowledge that nothing is impossible for Him:

> *"For nothing is impossible with God."* Luke 1:37 (New Living Translation).

We must all think at a much higher level when we pray because God is much greater than we can even imagine!

Action Step:

- Can you remember times, when you were so overwhelmed by the perceived immensity of your problems, that you almost felt bad to ask God for help?

- Make a commitment to never again talk about your "mountains of problems" as if they are a challenge for God. God looks down on mountains, not up! Get His perspective on things.

- Make a choice to elevate your thinking to the realm where nothing is impossible for God!

Review:

1. Prayer Is Simply Talking and Listening to God.

2. Prayer Should Flow from A Contrite Heart.

3. Your Prayers Should Be Confident.

4. Your Prayers Should Be Concise and To the Point.

5. Your Prayers Should Be Consistent and Constant.

6. Pray in Jesus' Name.

7. Pray About Everything!

8. You Do Not Have Because You Don't Ask God.

9. Asking God with The Wrong Motive Doesn't Work.

10. Ask Expecting to Receive from God.

11. Ask God to Bless Your Enemies as You Pray.

12. Ask the Lord to Make You More Loving as You Pray.

13. Make Talking to God a Priority Every Day.

14. Pray According to God's Will.

15. Prayer Frames Help Shape Our Prayers.

16. Ask God to Change the Way You Think.

17. Think at A Higher Level When You Pray.

DAY 18

Where the Mind Goes the Person Follows

"For as he thinks within himself, so he is."
Proverbs 23:7 (New American Standard Bible).

"For as he thinks in his heart, so is he."
Proverbs 23:7 (New King James Version).

The Bible is clear in its teaching: A person's thinking determines his or her reality. By implication, if you can change your thinking, you can change your life! We talked about the importance of thinking at a higher level when talking to God. We continue today by reinforcing that your thoughts determine your life. If you want to change your life, you must change your thinking.

Most of us end up talking to others about what we think about the most. What we talk about will ultimately shape our actions, attitudes and outcomes. Please understand that intentional thinking creates intended results.

Consider this for a moment: Your current situation is the result of yesterday's thoughts. Your current thoughts will influence tomorrow's results. If you are currently thinking a bunch of negative or angry thoughts, there is a good chance that it will spill over into negative words, attitudes and results! Where your thoughts lead, you will follow.

It is critical to take responsibility for your thoughts. Nobody else can be assigned to your thinking! You and only you can work on this area of your life. Your thinking cannot be delegated to an associate or family member. If you are negative, it will be hard to pray and ask God for a miracle. If you cannot ask for that miracle, your situation will remain as negative as your thinking. Thus, there you will be ... right where your negative thinking led you!

You may wonder how long and how often you should work at elevating your thinking. Personally, I believe you and I must work at it for as long as we live in this cynical world. No one is exempted. Instead of being overwhelmed by the prospect of a life-long vigilance regarding your thinking, be at peace. God is present to help you in your quest!

Commit to God and lean on Him to help you. Trust Him to carry you through your battles for positive thoughts:

> *"You will guard him and keep him in perfect and constant peace whose mind both its inclination and its character is stayed on You, because he commits himself to You, leans on You, and hopes confidently in You."* Isaiah 26:3 (Amplified Bible).

Where is your mind leading you? You can choose!

Action Step:

- If you continue your current train of thought, where will you end up?

- Make a conscious decision that you will become confident by agreeing with God's opinion of you.

- How can you adjust your thoughts to make room for God's miraculous intervention in your life?

- Start praying with higher expectation.

- Start living with greater gratitude.

- Start believing that you will receive everything you ask of the Lord!

Review:

1. Prayer Is Simply Talking and Listening to God.

2. Prayer Should Flow from A Contrite Heart.

3. Your Prayers Should Be Confident.

4. Your Prayers Should Be Concise and To the Point.

5. Your Prayers Should Be Consistent and Constant.

6. Pray in Jesus' Name.

7. Pray About Everything!

8. You Do Not Have Because You Don't Ask God.

9. Asking God with The Wrong Motive Doesn't Work.

10. Ask Expecting to Receive from God.

11. Ask God to Bless Your Enemies as You Pray.

12. Ask the Lord to Make You More Loving as You Pray.

13. Make Talking to God a Priority Every Day.

14. Pray According to God's Will.

15. Prayer Frames Help Shape Our Prayers.

16. Ask God to Change the Way You Think.

17. Think at A Higher Level When You Pray.

18. Where the Mind Goes The Person Follows.

DAY 19

Always Pray and Never Give Up

One day Jesus told his disciples a story to show that they should always pray and never give up. "There was a judge in a certain city," he said, "who neither feared God nor cared about people. A widow of that city came to him repeatedly, saying, 'Give me justice in this dispute with my enemy.' The judge ignored her for a while, but finally he said to himself, 'I don't fear God or care about people, but this woman is driving me crazy. I'm going to see that she gets justice, because she is wearing me out with her constant requests!'" Then the Lord said, "Learn a lesson from this unjust judge. Even he rendered a just decision in the end. So don't you think God will surely give justice to his chosen people who cry out to him day and night? Will he keep putting them off? I tell you, he will grant justice to them quickly! But when the Son of Man returns, how many will he find on the earth who have faith?" Luke 18:1-8 (New Living Translation).

This story serves to remind us that <u>perseverance in prayer will be rewarded</u> because <u>it takes faith to persevere</u>! God is not only attentive to the prayers of His people, but He also desires to give them the justice they crave. There is a lot of corrupt dealings in our world, and often God is the only refuge we can find as we suffer from injustice. However, when we allow the thinking of this world to invade our lives, it is easy to give up and stop believing God.

We must remind ourselves that <u>God rewards faith and that faith is often best revealed when the answer seems to be slow in coming.</u>

> *"And it is impossible to please God without faith. Anyone who wants to come to him must believe that God exists and that he rewards those who sincerely seek him."* Hebrews 11:6 (New Living Translation).

As you read through the faith chapter of Hebrews 11, you will see that many biblical heroes had to persevere through long seasons of waiting for their prayers to be answered.

> *"We do not want you to become lazy, but to <u>imitate</u> those who through faith and patience*

[handwritten margin note: utilize a prayer journal to remember to continue to pray for requests that take time for an answer]

inherit what has been promised." Hebrews 11:6 (New International Version).

God answers our prayers when we persevere through seasons of patient waiting. The widow obtained her answer from an unrighteous judge, and we will obtain our answers from the Righteous Judge in the same way. We must always pray, which takes faith, and we must never give up, which takes patience.

We receive what has been promised through prayer and perseverance!

Action Step:

- Have you given up on some of your prayer requests lately?

- Have you truly persevered in your prayers, or did you quit way too soon?

- Remember always to pray (faith) and never to give up (patience/perseverance)!

Review:

1. Prayer Is Simply Talking and Listening to God.

2. Prayer Should Flow from A Contrite Heart.

3. Your Prayers Should Be Confident.

4. Your Prayers Should Be Concise and To the Point.

5. Your Prayers Should Be Consistent and Constant.

6. Pray in Jesus' Name.

7. Pray About Everything!

8. You Do Not Have Because You Don't Ask God.

9. Asking God with The Wrong Motive Doesn't Work.

10. Ask Expecting to Receive from God.

11. Ask God to Bless Your Enemies as You Pray.

12. Ask the Lord to Make You More Loving as You Pray.

13. Make Talking to God a Priority Every Day.

14. Pray According to God's Will.

15. Prayer Frames Help Shape Our Prayers.

16. Ask God to Change the Way You Think.

17. Think at A Higher Level When You Pray.

18. Where the Mind Goes The Person Follows.

19. Always Pray and Never Give Up.

DAY 20

Ask God to Show You What You Need to See

"When the servant of the man of God got up early the next morning and went outside, there were troops, horses, and chariots everywhere. "Oh, sir, what will we do now?" the young man cried to Elisha. "Don't be afraid!" Elisha told him. "For there are more on our side than on theirs!" Then Elisha prayed, "O Lord, open his eyes and let him see!" The Lord opened the young man's eyes, and when he looked up, he saw that the hillside around Elisha was filled with horses and chariots of fire. As the Aramean army advanced toward him, Elisha prayed, "O Lord, please make them blind." So the Lord struck them with blindness as Elisha had asked. Then Elisha went out and told them, "You have come the wrong way! This isn't the right city! Follow me, and I will take you to the man you are looking for." And he led them to

the city of Samaria." 2 Kings 6:15-19 (New Living Translation).

How often do we feel like we are under attack, surrounded and utterly defeated by what we see with our natural eyes? This story reminds us that there is a spiritual world with spiritual realities unseen to the human eye. It is from that spiritual dimension that our salvation and provision will come when we call upon the Lord in prayer! We need to see that no matter how bad our situation gets, God is always able to rescue us and restore us!

> *"What shall we say about such wonderful things as these? If God is for us, who can ever be against us?"* Romans 8:31 NLT.

We need to see that there are more on our side than on theirs (those who oppose us in this world). Prayer can unlock our spiritual discernment and natural senses to become aware of God's work on our behalf. Prayer can likewise be used to lock up the senses of our enemies in this world, blinding them and giving us the victory!

Remind yourself not to be moved by what you see in the natural world around you. Ask God to show you and tell you that *"there are more on our side than on theirs."* Ask God to show you what you need to see.

Action Step:

- Have you felt like calamity surrounds you on every side? Are you feeling like the enemy is gaining on you and you have no hope?

- Ask God to show you in the Word how He surrounds you with angels and His love.

- Now pray like you are part of a victorious majority whose enemy is being led into an ambush of defeat!

- Take a moment to thank God for His amazing provision and protection.

Review:

1. Prayer Is Simply Talking and Listening to God.

2. Prayer Should Flow from A Contrite Heart.

3. Your Prayers Should Be Confident.

4. Your Prayers Should Be Concise and To the Point.

5. Your Prayers Should Be Consistent and Constant.

6. Pray in Jesus' Name.

7. Pray About Everything!

8. You Do Not Have Because You Don't Ask God.

9. Asking God with The Wrong Motive Doesn't Work.

10. Ask Expecting to Receive from God.

11. Ask God to Bless Your Enemies as You Pray.

12. Ask the Lord to Make You More Loving as You Pray.

13. Make Talking to God a Priority Every Day.

14. Pray According to God's Will.

15. Prayer Frames Help Shape Our Prayers.

16. Ask God to Change the Way You Think.

17. Think at A Higher Level When You Pray.

18. Where the Mind Goes The Person Follows.

19. Always Pray and Never Give Up.

20. Ask God to Show You What You Need to See.

IANN SCHONKEN

DAY 21

Lean into God's Strength with Your Weaknesses

"There is therefore now no condemnation to those who are in Christ Jesus, who do not walk according to the flesh, but according to the Spirit." Romans 8:1 (New King James Version).

One of the biggest challenges of being a believer is that we are still living in a fallen world. Our weaknesses and shortcomings are very evident as we come into God's perfect presence to worship and pray. However, we must remember that the Holy Spirit is right there to help us in our moments of weakness! It is easy to give in to the temptation to buckle under the weight of the condemnation we feel from the enemy. Remember, he is known as "the accuser of the brethren." There will always be a strong opposition to our mission of coming to God with our prayers on a regular basis. We will do well to remember the words of the apostle Paul to the Corinthian believers:

> *"Each time he said, "My grace is all you need. My power works best in weakness." So now I am glad to boast about my weaknesses, so that the power of Christ can work through me. That's why I take pleasure in my weaknesses, and in the insults, hardships, persecutions, and troubles that I suffer for Christ. For when I am weak, then I am strong."* 2 Corinthians 12:9-10 NLT

We have come to the end of our twenty-one days of prayer. My prayer is that you will gain strength from the fact that when you are weak, feeling overwhelmed by trials and tribulations and limping from the searing condemnation of your enemy, you can come into God's presence. You can rest assured of His acceptance, power, and grace as you reach out to Him in prayer. He will not turn away from you, but He will embrace you with His love:

> *"Come close to God, and God will come close to you."* James 4:8 NLT.

Remember this: You can lean into God's strength with all your weaknesses!

Action Step:

- Have you ever felt like you are just too bad of a person to come to God in prayer?

- Remember that condemnation is a weapon in the hands of our enemy, who will do anything to keep us isolated from God.

- Have you ever felt weak in your walk with God? Know that every weakness is an excellent opportunity to approach God for help. A spring in the desert breaks through the most vulnerable spot in the soil above it. In a similar way, God wants to spring up like a fountain through your place of weakness to water your desert moments.

- Take a moment to thank God for your weaknesses and your utter dependence on Him. Then ask Him to work with His power in your weakness!

- Please don't stop praying. God is ready to receive you wherever and whenever you call upon Him. He will welcome you even when you feel weak and condemned!

- Now that you have received these simple prayer principles, please continue to live by these principles going forward. Remember, you are a simple prayer away from God's reassuring presence!

- May God bless you with His peace and increase!

Review:

1. Prayer Is Simply Talking and Listening to God.

2. Prayer Should Flow from A Contrite Heart.

3. Your Prayers Should Be Confident.

4. Your Prayers Should Be Concise and To the Point.

5. Your Prayers Should Be Consistent and Constant.

6. Pray in Jesus' Name.

7. Pray About Everything!

8. You Do Not Have Because You Don't Ask God.

9. Asking God with The Wrong Motive Doesn't Work.

10. Ask Expecting to Receive from God.

11. Ask God to Bless Your Enemies as You Pray.

12. Ask the Lord to Make You More Loving as You Pray.

13. Make Talking to God a Priority Every Day.

14. Pray According to God's Will.

15. Prayer Frames Help Shape Our Prayers.

16. Ask God to Change the Way You Think.

17. Think at A Higher Level When You Pray.

18. Where the Mind Goes The Person Follows.

19. Always Pray and Never Give Up.

20. Ask God to Show You What You Need to See.

21. Lean into God's Strength with Your Weaknesses.

IANN SCHONKEN

About the Author

In 1988, Iann Schonken came to the United States from his country of birth, South Africa, to complete his college education. During this time, he served as an associate pastor in Ridgecrest, CA.

After receiving his Master's degree in Religion (Church Leadership), he went on to assist various evangelistic ministries in over a decade of ministry, administration, traveling, speaking and consultation.

In 1996, Iann went full-time on the road as a traveling and crusade evangelist in the United States, Brazil. Mozambique, Swaziland, Madagascar, India, the Philippines, Israel, Canada, and Australia.

From 2002-2006, he assisted Pastor Benny Perez in launching a church plant in Las Vegas, NV. Recently, he co-authored *myPrayerPartner: A Systematic Approach to Prayer,* and created *The School of Prayer* with his brother, Dr. Johann Schonken.

Iann has over twenty-five years of ministry experience and ministers the Word with great boldness and compassion, expecting signs and wonders to follow. Iann Schonken became Lead Pastor at Family Fellowship in October 2006 where he still serves today. He has been married for over twenty-four years to his wife Melodi, and is the grateful father of three boys.

His website is at:

http://www.iannschonken.com

45266120R00072

Made in the USA
San Bernardino, CA
04 February 2017